JÁNOS PILINSZKY

PASSIO

Fourteen Poems

Translated from the Hungarian
by Clive Wilmer and George Gömöri

First published in 2011 by
Worple Press
PO Box 328
Tonbridge
Kent TN9 1WR
www.worplepress.co.uk

Cover image by Charlotte Chisholm

Printed by imprintdigital
Upton Pyne, Exeter
www.imprintdigital.net

Typeset by narrator
www.narrator.me.uk
enquiries@narrator.me.uk

ISBN: 978-1-905208-14-2

Acknowledgements

Poems in this collection have previously appeared in the following periodicals: *Hungarian Quarterly*, *Poetry* and *Modern Poetry in Translation*. Thanks are due to the editors.

Contents

Introduction

János Pilinszky (1921-81) is one of the great European poets of an extraordinary generation: that of Paul Celan, Zbigniew Herbert and Yves Bonnefoy. Like them he grew up to a world physically and morally devastated by the Second World War and the Holocaust. He wrote about these things from direct experience. As a conscript in the Hungarian army, he was stationed in Southern Germany during the last years of the war. There he witnessed Allied prisoners-of-war at the point of starvation and seems also to have glimpsed a concentration camp.

Returning to his native Hungary at the conclusion of hostilities, he began to write and to publish. He was never prolific and the poems came slowly. The early ones are highly personal: intensely anguished explorations of identity and sexuality. It was not until his second book, *Harmadnapon* (On the Third Day), published in 1959, that he began to deal openly with his memories of the war. The personality which emerges from both the early books is of someone for whom the mere possibility of human suffering is almost intolerable, whose nerves are on the surface of his skin. There is something naked and innocent in the language, as if he could not forget his surprise at the horrors of existence. This vulnerability and what I can only describe as the enduring shock of a remembered historical moment chime with the sense of 'given-ness' in Existentialist thought – as if the poet had been dropped into the world and was startled by what he found there. Readers may be reminded of Giacometti or Beckett, though the key influences seem to have been the aphorisms of Simone Weil, the novels of Dostoevsky and the paintings of Van Gogh, all three understood as Christian Existentialists.

Pilinszky went on to publish five more books and became relatively famous in Hungary. Three selections have appeared in English: *Selected Poems*, translated by Ted Hughes and János Csokits (Carcanet, 1976 – later expanded as *The Desert of Love*

1

(Anvil, 1989)); *Crater*, translated by Peter Jay (Anvil, 1978); and an American publication, *Metropolitan Icons*, translated by Emery George (Edwin Mellen, 1995), which includes the Hungarian text. The war poems are prominent in the Hughes/Csokits selection; both Jay and George attempt some broadening of the picture, but good as Pilinszky's work in general is, the war poems are his overwhelming achievement. The later work is even more condensed and enigmatic than that in the early books, but it is somehow less immediate. In this short collection, therefore, we have concentrated on *Harmadnapon*, though poems from other books have been included.

I translate from Hungarian in collaboration with George Gömöri, whom I first met in 1971. A Hungarian poet himself, he is thirteen years younger than Pilinszky and belongs to the generation that felt his influence. Over the past forty years Gömöri and I have translated work by more than twenty poets and introduced British readers to the poems of Miklós Radnóti and György Petri. Like Gömöri, I admired Pilinszky from early on, but we made no attempt to translate him for many years, having been forestalled by Ted Hughes – not a poet one wants to compete with. When the Hughes/Csokits *Selected Poems* first appeared, I have to say, I reviewed it unfavourably. It means more to me today than it did then, but I remain not quite content with it. Hughes conveys Pilinszky's images, his nervous anguish and something of his visionary quality with memorable power, but at the cost of abandoning the poetry's cultural halo. For instance, as Gömöri points out, the line I render as 'Their neighbours' fallen flesh' in 'Harbach 1944' (p. 6) has Christian resonances, but Hughes's plainer translation – 'the falling bodies of their companions' – presents it as a simple matter of fact. Moreover, Hughes ignores Pilinszky's rhyme and metre, which are in my view crucial to his meaning and to the austerely disciplined effect of the *Harmadnapon* poems. (The later poems, such as 'One Fine Day', p. 19, are mostly in free verse and it is partly the absence of metre that accounts for their fainter impact.) More or less balladic in convention, the form calls to mind the impersonal grimness of folk poetry: as perhaps in such English poems as Blake's 'London' and Coleridge's 'Ancient Mariner', which in my versions served me as points of reference. It was our differences with Hughes and Csokits that finally led us to try translating Pilinszky. We wanted to see if a Pilinszky more consciously rooted in tradition could be put across in English. As soon as we started work, I discovered the sort of difficulty that our rivals must have encountered before us. It has something to do with Pilinszky's evident honesty, which finds an equivalent in the exactness of his technique. One feels that this is a poet who could not posture or tell a lie in his poems, which means – strange though it may seem – that he is difficult to translate: more so than any poet I have attempted. The language of his poems is so economical and the straightforward metres so precise that they offer the translator no openings for paraphrase. Every syllable counted. Hungarian is normally more expansive than English, but in spite of that, I often found myself having to cut things from the originals to achieve my versions of Pilinszky's stanza forms. At the same time, I found it much easier to put across the complex matter of such a poem as 'The French Prisoner' (p. 8) within the architecture of a formal stanza than it is when the verse has no objective discipline. In the Hughes/Csokits version this greatly lucid poem verges on obscurity, which it shouldn't.

But we do not offer these versions as definitive, nor are they representative. They are not just the poems we wanted to translate but also the ones that didn't completely defeat us. They constitute an approach to a poet not unknown in the English-speaking world, who deserves to be regarded as seminal and, notwithstanding the modesty of his work, as one of the major poets of modern times.

Clive Wilmer
Cambridge, 2011

3

On a Forbidden Star

I was born on a forbidden star. From there
driven ashore, I trudge along the sand.
The surf of celestial nothingness takes me up,
and plays with me, then casts me on the land.

Why I repent I do not even know.
It is a puzzle buzzing in my ear.
If any of you should find me on this beach,
this sunken beach, don't run away, stay here.

And don't be scared. Don't run away. Just try
to mitigate the suffering in my life.
Shut your eyes and press me to yourself.
Press me boldly, as you would a knife.

Be reckless too: look on me as the dead
look on the night, seeing it as their own,
your shoulder there to aid my weaker one.
I can no longer bear to be alone.

I never wanted to be born. It was nothingness
Who bore and suckled me; with her I started.
So love me darkly. Love me cruelly. Love me
like the one left behind by the departed.

Harbach 1944

I keep on seeing them: a shaft
rears and the moon is full –
there are men harnessed to the shaft.
It's a huge cart they pull.

They are dragging a massive wagon,
which grows as the night does,
their bodies split between the claims
of hunger, trembling, dust.

They bear the road, the horizon,
the beet fields shivering,
but only feel the burdening land,
the weight of everything.

Their neighbours' fallen flesh
seems stuck into their own,
as in each other's tracks they sway,
to living layers grown.

Villages keep clear of them
and gates avoid their feet.
The distances approaching them
falter and retreat.

Staggering, they wade knee-deep
in the dark, muffled sound
of clattering clogs, as if unseen
leaves carpeted the ground.

Silence accepts their frames. Each face
is dipped in height, as if
straining for the scent of troughs
in the sky far off.

And like a cattle-yard prepared
for the herded beasts outside –
its gates flung open violently –
death, for them, gapes wide.

The French Prisoner

If only I could forget him, the Frenchman
I saw outside our quarters, creeping round
near daybreak in that density of garden
as if he'd almost grown into the ground.
He was just looking back, peering about him
to check that he was safe here and alone:
once he was sure, his plunder was all his!
Whatever chanced, he'd not be moving on.

He was already eating. He was wolfing
a pilfered turnip hidden in his rags.
Eating raw cattle feed. But he'd no sooner
swallowed a mouthful than it made him gag;
and the sweet food encountered on his tongue
delight and then disgust, as it might be
the unhappy and the happy, meeting in
their bodies' all-consuming ecstasy.

Only forget that body … Shoulder blades
trembling, and a hand all skin and bone,
the palm cramming his mouth in such a way
that it too seemed to feed in clinging on.
And then the furious and desperate shame
of organs galled with one another, forced
to tear from one another what should bind them
together in community at last.

The way his clumsy feet had been left out
of all that gibbering bestial joy; and how
they stood splayed out and paralysed beneath
the body's torture and fierce rapture now.

And his look too – if I could forget that!
Retching, he went on gobbling as if driven
on and on, just to eat, no matter what,
anything, this or that, himself even.

Why go on? It turned out that he'd escaped
from the prison camp nearby – guards came for him.
I wander, as I did then in that garden,
among my garden shadows here at home.
'If only I could forget him, the Frenchman' –
I'm looking through my notes, I read one out,
and from my ears, my eyes, my mouth, the seething
memory boils over in his shout:

'I'm hungry!' And immediately I feel
the undying hunger which this wretched creature
has long since ceased to feel, for which there is
no mitigating nourishment in nature.
He feeds on me. More and more hungrily!
And I'm less and less sufficient, for my part.
Now he, who would have been contented once
with any kind of food, demands my heart.

The Passion at Ravensbrück

One steps clear of the others, stands
in a block of silence, still.
The prison garb, the convict's scalp
blink like an old film-reel.

Fearful to be a self alone:
the pores are visible,
with everything around so huge
and everything so small.

And that was it. As for the rest –
for the rest, without a sound,
simply forgetting to cry out,
the body hit the ground.

The Desert of Love

A bridge, a scorching asphalt road.
Emptying its pockets, one by one
the day sets its possessions out.
In the catatonic dusk you are alone.

The landscape's like a trench's wrinkled floor.
Scars sparkle in the twilight glow and glimmer.
It's darkening. Brilliance stuns you and the sun
strikes you blind. I can't forget that summer.

A summer storm with lightning at white heat.
There are, like blazing cherubim, winged creatures,
that stand without a feather fluttering
in cages boarded up and thorned with splinters.

Do you remember it? First came the wind;
then there was earth; then, the cooping box.
Fire and dung. And once in a while, too,
a few wing-beats and then an empty reflex.

And thirst. And then it was I asked for water.
I hear my fevered gulping, even today,
and helpless as a stone I must endure it,
and blow the dazzle and mirage away.

Years go by, years, and hope is now no more
than a tin cup upset in the dry straw.

11

On the Wall of a KZ Lager

Where you've fallen, you will stay.
In the whole universe this one
and only place is the sole place
which you have made your very own.

The country runs away from you.
House, mill, poplar – every thing
is struggling with you here, as if
in nothingness mutating.

But now it's you who won't give up.
Did we fleece you? You've grown rich.
Did we blind you? You watch us still.
You bear witness without speech.

Quatrain

Nails sleep in icy sand. A night
of posters drenched in loneliness.
The light outside, you left that on.
It is today they pierce my flesh.

For a Portrait

The sun cools in the pencilled dusk.
In my face there's a numb sea gleaming;
it has depths, it has wide expanses.
I am old. I believe in nothing.

I am old: in my ruined features
just the watery waste, which is terrible,
and the granite dust of twilight. Just
a lacework of pores like a harsh veil.

Waves crashing. Then the unhappy noises
of the soft night. Blind insect on the stage
of a cardboard box that darkens around me,
I'm alone in this world-wide orphanage.

And alone in a bed that's bottomless.
Alone among pillows, tossed back and forth.
Alone in unending loneliness.
Like the sea. Like Mother Earth.

The Just-Past

For Ted Hughes

It arrives, and it goes rigid.
On the still, ashen wall it sits:
the moon. A single, massive blow.
A deathly silence is the core of it.

It shatters roads, the moonshine;
makes them all tremble, crack.
It tears this wall apart, the white
pouring across black.

The black day's rent by lightning,
and lightning, and more lightning. Here,
there is white pouring down, and also black.
In a magnetic storm you comb your hair.

You comb your hair in a mirror more alert
than the just-past, in a silence drenched in light.

You sit there in your silence, combing
your hair in the mirror, as if in a glass coffin.

November Elysium

A time for convalescence. You stop short
at the garden gate. You have the cloistered silence
of a still, yellow wall as your background.
A light breeze rises gently from the herbs
and now, as if annealed with holy oil,
the five tormented wounds that are your senses,
soothed, begin to heal.

You're timid and exultant. Yes. And pausing
with childishly translucent arms and legs
in a greatcoat and shawl, both overgrown,
you are like Alyosha Karamazov.

And also like the meek, like those who come
as children, yes, and happy like a child
as well, for you want nothing any more.
Only to glow in the November sun
and give off fragrance light as a fir-cone's.
Only to bask in sunlight like the blest.

Introitus

Who will open the book which is now closed?
Who make the first cut into unbroken time?
Turning the pages over, dawn to dawn,
lifting the pages up, casting them down?

Who of us dares reach into the furnace
of the not-yet-known? Who furthermore would dare
search through the dense leaves of the sealed book?
And who is there to do so with hands bare?

And who of us is not afraid? Who'd not be
when God himself has shut his eyes, and when
the angels all fall down before his face,
and when his creatures darken, every one?

The Lamb, alone of us, is not afraid,
he only, who was slain: the Lamb who (look!)
now comes clattering over the glass sea
and mounts the throne. And then, opens the book.

17

Van Gogh's Prayer

A battle lost in the cornfields
and in the sky a victory.
Birds, the sun and birds again.
By night, what will be left of me?

By night, only a row of lamps,
a wall of yellow clay that shines,
and down the garden, through the trees,
like candles in a row, the panes;

there I dwelt once and dwell no longer –
I can't live where I once lived, though
the roof there used to cover me.
Lord, you covered me long ago.

One Fine Day

I've always been after the thrown-away tin spoon
and the tawdry landscapes of misery,
hoping that one fine day
I'd be overwhelmed by sobbing, that the old
courtyard would gently take me back, with the ivied
silence and whisperings of home.

I have always longed,
always been longing
for home.

Before

I don't know much about the future, but
I can picture the Last Judgement.
That day, that hour
will be the exaltation of our nakedness.

No one will look for another in the multitude.
The Cross, as if but a splinter,
will be taken back into the Father,
and the angels, creatures of heaven,
will lay open the world's last page.
And then we'll say: *I love you.* We'll say:
I love you very much. And in the sudden pushing and shoving
our cries will free the waters once again,
before we sit down at the table.